This Notebook Belongs To:

live
MORE
worry
LESS

Time to head back to
Amazon to order
another book. If you
enjoyed this notebook,
we hope you will
share your opinion
by leaving a review
on Amazon.
Thank you,
Inspired Lines

www.ingramcontent.com/pod-product-compliance
Lightning Source LLC
Chambersburg PA
CBHW070612220526
45467CB00003B/1390

* 9 7 8 1 7 0 7 2 5 6 2 7 3 *